DRAWING WITH Sports Illustrated KIDS

PICTURE A TOUCHDOWN

A Football Drawing Book

by Anthony Wacholtz

illustrated by Mike Ray

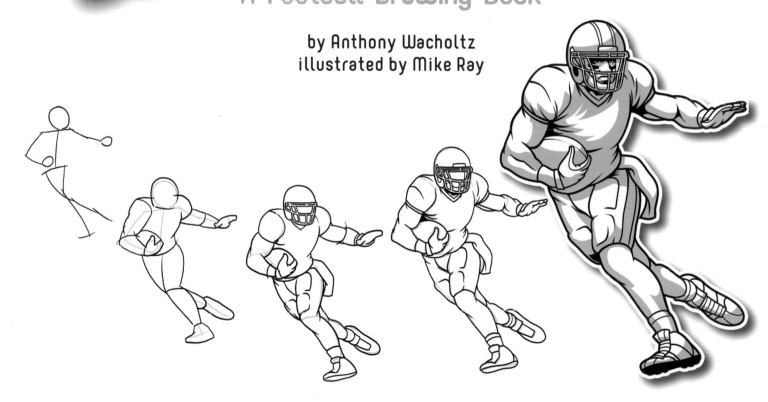

CAPSTONE PRESS
a capstone imprint

TABLE OF CONTENTS

It's First and 10 (and Time to Draw!)

It's time to put on your pads, throw on your helmet, and start drawing! Let Sports Illustrated Kids be your guide as you draw yourself into the action on the football field. Are you ready to throw a perfect spiral? Or would you rather make a crushing tackle? But what's more exciting than pulling in the winning touchdown catch? If you can't decide, draw them all!

Follow the simple step-by-step drawings in this book, and you'll be on your way to football stardom. Before you know it, you'll be part of the game. Let's get started!

Before you head out on the field, grab some supplies:

1. First you'll need drawing paper. Any type of blank, unlined paper will do.

2. Pencils are the easiest to use for your drawing projects. Make sure you have plenty of them.

3. It's easier to make clean lines with sharpened pencils. Keep a pencil sharpener close by.

4. As you practice drawing, you'll need a good eraser. Pencil erasers wear out very quickly. Get a rubber or kneaded eraser.

5. When your drawing is finished, you can trace over it with a black ink pen or a thin felt-tip marker. The dark lines will make your drawing jump off the page.

6. If you decide to color your drawings, colored pencils and markers usually work best. You can also use colored pencils to shade your drawings and make them more lifelike.

MAKING THE PASS

You drop back to pass and see an open receiver downfield. You'll have to fire off the pass before you get sacked!

1

AIMING DOWNFIELD

You've got plenty of time. Your offensive line is keeping the defensive linemen at bay. You bring your hand back and prepare to throw a perfect spiral.

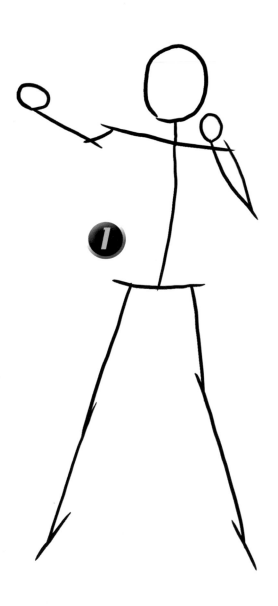

QB SCRAMBLE

The pocket has collapsed! You'll have to scramble. Let's hope you can buy enough time for a receiver to get open!

BREAK THROUGH THE LINE

You find a hole in the line and start to race through. You make a cut as defenders miss their tackles. What a move!

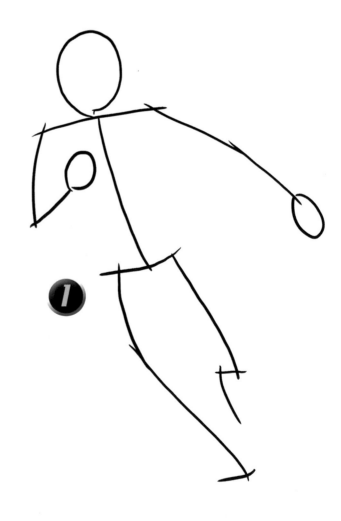

1

④

STIFF-ARM

There's only one defender left to beat, but he's right on top of you. Get ready to stiff-arm him!

1

4

Open Field Run

Zoom! You streak down the field, leaving everyone in your dust. There's only one question left: What will your touchdown dance look like?

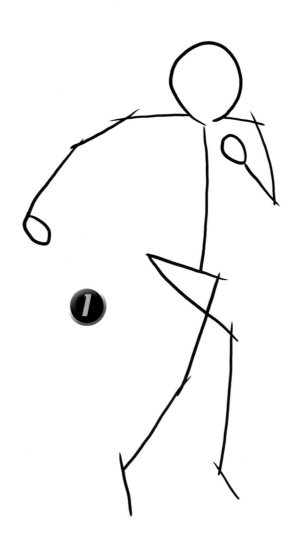

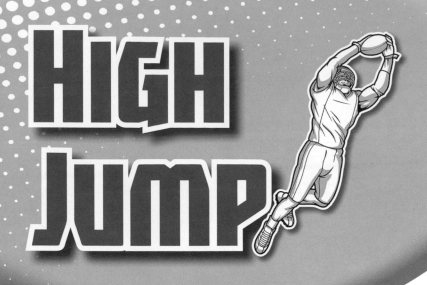

HIGH JUMP

Here comes the pass! It's a little high, but that hasn't stopped you before. You leap for the pass, securing the ball with both hands.

1

RIGHT ON TARGET

You run your route and beat your defender. You turn your head just as the pass drops in front of you. Perfect timing!

TD DIVE

You're so close! The end zone is yards away. You dive forward with your arms stretched out, trying to carry the ball over the goal line. Touchdown!

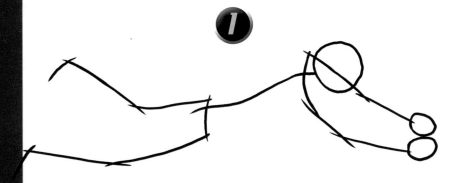

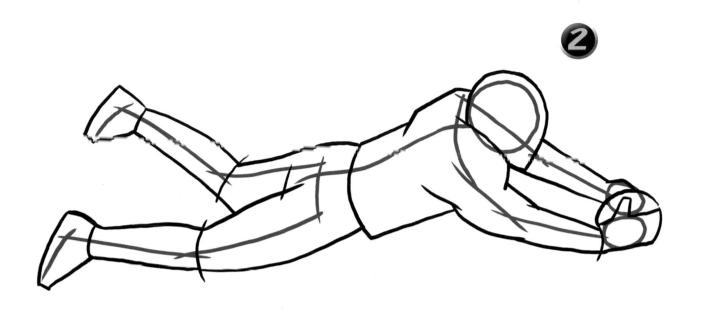

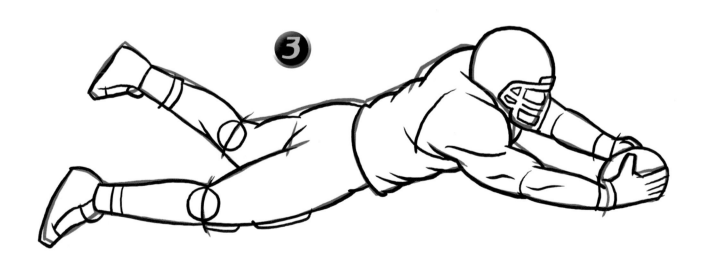

⑤

ALL EYES ON YOU

You've scored a touchdown, and it's your moment in the spotlight. How will you celebrate?

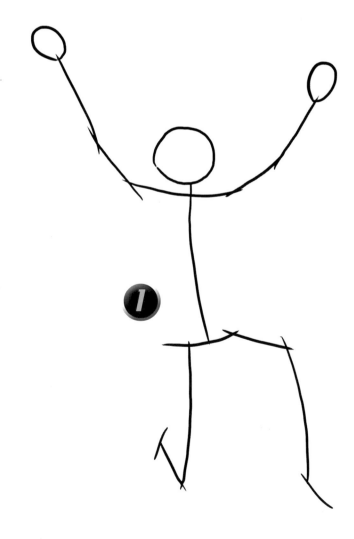

4

One on One

You're matched up against the opponent's fastest receiver. If he gets into the open field, you could be in trouble. You'd better get up to the line of scrimmage to slow him down.

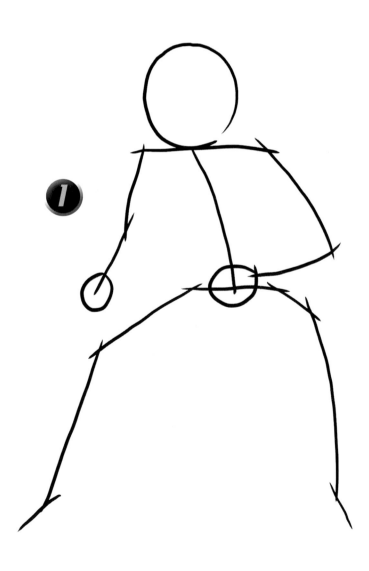

WRAPPED UP

The running back isn't going anywhere! Just as he hits his stride, you send him flying backward with a powerful tackle. They won't run that play again!

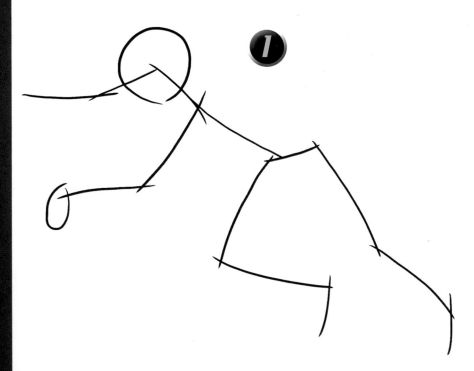

PICK OFF THE PASS

You've read the quarterback's eyes perfectly—the ball's going to your receiver. With a few quick steps, you launch into the air. You've got the position, the higher jump, and now the ball. Interception!

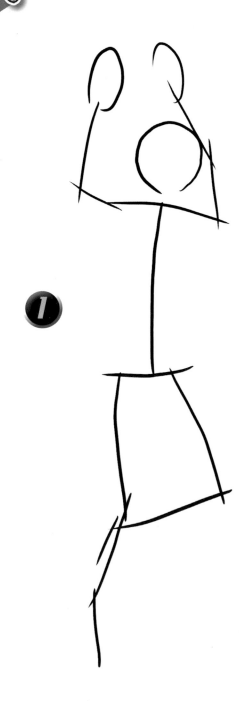

1

BLOCK THE PUNT

It's fourth down for the other team, and the punter has come on the field. But not so fast! As he steps forward to kick, you sprint in from the outside and throw your hand up to block the punt.

1

GIVE IT A BOOT

Your team didn't get the first down, so you run onto the field to punt. With a good kick, you can pin the other team back near its own end zone.

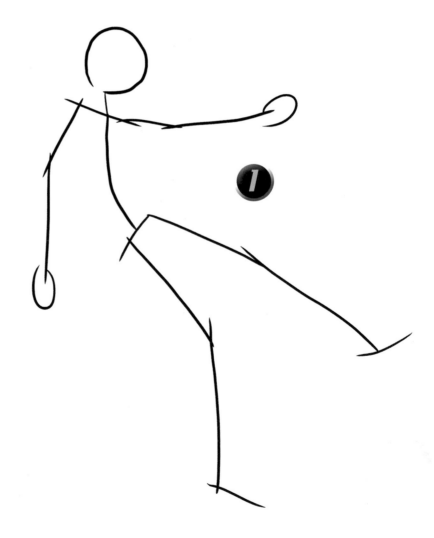

1

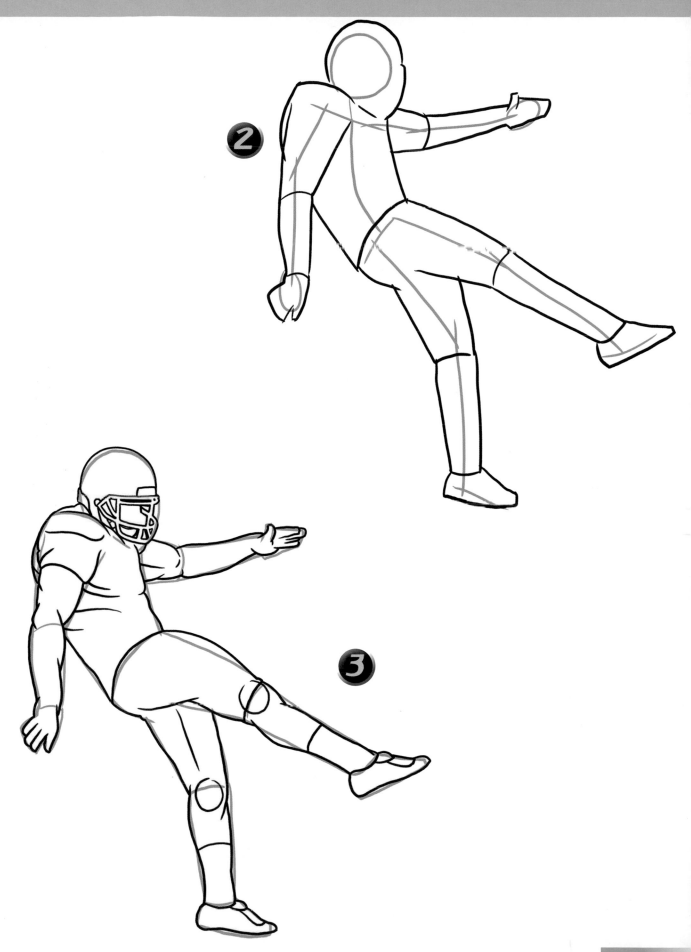

READ MORE

Ames, Lee J. *Draw 50 Athletes: The Step-by-Step Way to Draw Wrestlers and Figure Skaters, Baseball and Football Players, and Many More.* 2nd ed. New York: Watson Guptill, 2012.

Biskup, Agnieszka. *Football: How It Works.* Sports Illustrated Kids. Mankato, Minn.: Capstone Press, 2010.

Frederick, Shane. *The Ultimate Collection of Pro Football Records.* Sports Illustrated Kids. North Mankato, Minn.: Capstone Press, 2013.

INTERNET SITES

FactHound offers a safe, fun way to find Internet sites related to this book. All of the sites on FactHound have been researched by our staff.

Here's all you do:

Visit *www.facthound.com*

Type in this code: 9781476531045

Super-cool stuff! Check out projects, games and lots more at **www.capstonekids.com**

TITLES IN THIS SERIES:

Drawing with Sports Illustrated Kids is published by Capstone Press, 1710 Roe Crest Drive, North Mankato, Minnesota 56003
www.capstonepub.com

Library of Congress Cataloging-in-Publication Data
Wacholtz, Anthony.
  Picture a touchdown : a football drawing book / by Anthony Wacholtz.
  pages cm.—(Sports illustrated kids. Drawing with sports illustrated kids)
  ISBN 978-1-4765-3104-5 (library binding)
  1. Football—Juvenile literature. I. Title.
GV950.7.W34 2014
796.332—dc23   2013006660

Editorial Credits
Tracy Davies McCabe, designer; Eric Gohl, media researcher; Eric Manske, production specialist

Photo Credits
Sports Illustrated: Al Tielemans, cover, 11, 15, 23, 43, 55, 59, Bob Rosato, 35, 47, 51, David E. Klutho, 63, John Biever, 19, Peter Read Miller, 27, Simon Bruty, 7, 31, 39

Printed in the United States of America in North Mankato, Minnesota.
032013   007223CGF13